# BALEFIRE

Amy,

With admiration for you,
your compassion for the world,
and the bright depths of
your art. May Montana
be a kind of blessing
to you & your family.

Shann

# BALEFIRE

*poems*
## Shann Ray

LOST HORSE PRESS
Sandpoint, Idaho

# ACKNOWLEDGEMENTS

I would like to thank the editors of the magazines and other venues where the following poems have appeared:

*Best New Poets*: "A Quiet Poem about Marital Sex" (open competition winner)
*Black and White Journal for the Arts*: "The Gesture" and "Mystic Lake, The Beartooth Range"
*Borderlands*: "Icarus, USA"
*Poetry*: "My Dad, in America"
*Poetry Daily*: "My Dad, in America"
*Poetry International*: "The Violence Elegies: He Rides," "The Stockman Bar" and "The
    Wellington Hotel"
*Portland Review*: "Up Going to the Sun Road . . ."
*Ruminate*: "Invocation"

"The Hunter's Son" from the sequence "East of the Bear's Paw Mountains, North of Milk River" was the winner of the *Poetry Quarterly* Rebecca Lard Award; "My Dad, in America" was a finalist for the *Ruminate* Poetry Prize; "The Suicide Elegies"—"After the Dead Say What They Want," "After a Curse Against Elegies," "After Angels of the Love Affair," "After the Fallen Angels," and "After Despair and Courage"—won the *Subterrain* Poetry Prize.

*Author photo:* Vanessa Kay
*Book & Cover design by* Christine Holbert

This and other lost horse press titles may be viewed online at www.losthorsepress.org.

FIRST EDITION

LIBRARY OF CONGRESS CATALOGING-IN-PUBLICATION DATA
Ray, Shann.
    [Poems. Selections]
    Balefire : poems / by Shann Ray.—First Edition.
        pages cm
    ISBN 978-0-9911465-1-2 (alk. paper)
    I. Title.
    PS3618.A9828A6 2014
    811'.6—dc23
                        2013045676

 *for Jennifer*

*What is to give light must endure burning.*

—Anton Wildgans

*Ite inflammate omnia.*

—Ignatius de Loyola

# TABLE OF CONTENTS

## I

## II

## III

# VII

## IF YOU WALK TO SUNRIFT GORGE
## OR AVALANCHE LAKE

or just drive up Going to the Sun Road in late June, July,
the wildflowers like so many coveted women

or like my wife, self-possessed
and funny enough to call herself the hand of God

will take you and make you forget
the pain in this world.

I am not afraid to ask you why you trace my outline
with your fingertips, or why your hands mirror mine

or why we are clothed in the garment of praise
instead of despair,

the perfect iris of your eye
haloed black, wild like the mountain.

# MY DAD, IN AMERICA

Your hand on my jaw
        but gently

and that picture
of you punching through snow
          to bring two deer, a gopher,

and a magpie
          to the old Highwalker woman

who spoke only Cheyenne
          and traced our footprints

on leather she later chewed to soften.
          We need to know in America there is still blood

for forgiveness.
Dead things for the new day.

# THE VIOLENCE ELEGIES

### *He Rides*

bulls in every rodeo he can find.
Every Saturday night

he fights in bars. Takes off his shirt
to counter hand holds. Doesn't drink, tries not to

when fighting. Seeks only the concave feel of facial structure,
the slippery skin of cheekbones,

the line of a man's jaw
and the cool sockets of the eyes.

He likes especially
the sound these make

as they give way, the sound
of cartilage and how the skin slits open

before the blood begins,
the white-hard glisten of bone, the sound

of the face when it breaks.
And he hears as if from the quiet

eye of a child's dream,
his mother saying come home.

## The Stockman Bar

Montana, 1933 or today, he is seated on the ground, knees in his arms
    in front of the Mercantile in a new town, looking

for work. He will rise, cross the dirt street, approach the front door
    of the Stockman, black door, oiled hinges, inside

a dim small room and tables. Dark marble counter with five stools,
    clean. A lone bartender wipes things down.

Help you? the tender says. No, the man needs a chair
    to sit in, a space to calm his mind. The bartender

spits in a tin cup on the counter. Don't drink, don't stay, he says,
    and the man feels himself shutting down, his insides heavy

and tight, the center of him like an eclipse that obscures the light,
    three quick steps and a fist that rides the force of hip and shoulder:

the tender laid cold on the hardwood floor. Not dead,
    but still, and flatbacked. The man seated in the chair he desired

watching the blood curl from a three-inch line over the bartender's eye
    elliptic down his face to his neck to the floor.
    Orbital bone still sound.

## The Wellington Hotel

In the half-dark in the basement of a bar outside White Sulfur he opens
     the sphere of a man's head

on the corner of a table. The man's brothers, the man's friends
     gather seeking revenge. He throws

them back and breaks teeth
from the mouth of one. He pins another

against the wall, snaps
     the collarbone. You'll leave here dead

he says, and the group recedes,
     the power in him hungry

like winterkill, glistening, unkempt, the young,
     the old, and he walks from the open door

alone into darkness until he sits off distant watching a spider move
     in a quick circle around his boot,

a blackbird tilt
     on the wire near his neck.

## NIGHT OVER THE SAPPHIRE RANGE
## EAST OF MISSOULA

Tomorrow you lead the people
in praise
but tonight
in the quiet of our bedroom
silver birds fly
from your mouth
and break me all the way down.

How good it is to be
a vessel for the song
of this house of dawn.

Cup my hand to your hipbone
and give me darkness through the window.

# THE SUICIDE ELEGIES

—for Anne Sexton

## *After the Dead Say What They Want*

When her father falls asleep she wonders
at his presence here. She leaves him
for the kitchen and the drawer next to the sink
where she lifts the straight-knife for cutting vegetables,
considers the black slits of her eyes
peering from the side of the blade. This knife
is something she owns, so she takes it, her own heavy object, back

to her bedroom. She places his suit coat and gloves on the floor,
sits down at the vanity, another something,
another heaviness, this furniture, tangible, physical, another thing
she has not lost. In the mirror she finds her face, without makeup,
like an oil painting of earth and darkness,
pale hues underlined in black and grey, off-white, dark brown,
like soil, like sky when there is no sky, thick clouds so full

even breathing feels foreign, her fingers like mallets
hard against her face so the bones ache and weariness takes her
to where everything one day
must fall. I'm crazy, she thinks, and walks
to the bathroom, runs a hot bath and slides beneath the surface
and comes to rest. Rising, she
reaches the knife and cuts both wrists to the bone.

### After a Curse Against Elegies

When he wakes all he sees is water,
and he doesn't hear her. In the bathroom,
her limp form, vacant eyes. Frozen, he trembles, gasps. Please,
he whispers. Sees the wounds on her wrists. Fumbling,
he removes his own socks and ties them
over the openings, over gashes that look otherworldly
and warlike, ravaged, like diseased eyes or mouths,

and he is talking out loud now. Stay here!
Please stay. But she is unconscious as he throws the bedspread
over her, and wraps her like an infant, lifting her as he forces his feet
into his shoes. He runs to his car, the interstate, the hospital,
to a steel table where medical servants pump blood to her veins
and stitch her skin so that her bones subdue and she is asleep,

finally, him seated in the chair
beside her. He holds her hand, his head
like an anvil, face down. Tears run
dry. His body empty. Broken. Still.
Prayers lost like sheep in the dark
of his dreams. Sleep comes,
unwanted, all-consuming.

When she wakes she sees him
and thinks now everyone has died,
and this again is where they meet, in white rooms
made with pillows and wires, and light so bright there is no darkness.
She touches his hair, sees her arms bandaged and bound, and
when she touches his face, she feels almost visible, almost real
though weightless, lighter than air, and she knows

now what she wants. Her eyelids descend. She sleeps.
Two nurses, a male, thick-jawed and heavy,
a female with birdlike bones, stand in the doorway
and speak in hushed tones.
Shame, the man whispers. Shakes his head. He's seen it often
but still he finds it strange, and overdone, the violence,
the wilderness, he thinks, of the human mind.

*After Angels of the Love Affair*

Understandable, the woman says, and sees herself
walking in her own desires, lonely when she leaves the hospital
after dark, life so painfully minute, and death so large, like an ocean,
limitless and singular, so precise, but without end, unbound
by earth or atmosphere, no more pain, and the vision comes,
as it often does, of grey birds flying the border between this world
and the next, the tonal whisper of wings, musical and foreign,

welcoming her. When the father wakes he sees his daughter's
sleeping face, the short breaths she takes. How lovely she is,
he admits, and he is shocked at his desperateness, how much he hopes.
At her wedding he was barely aware when she spoke
in his ear, viciously, in the receiving line, You are a terrible man.
Selfish. Uncaring. He wants and doesn't want to say how right she was,
how poor a man he is, has always been, like most men,

same poverty of mind, same darkness.
Hidden, unknowable. I tried, he says aloud as she sleeps.
But he knows he didn't. Her mother did, he thinks.
Dead now, ovarian cancer. A deeply interior disease
probably symbolic of his disloyalty. He hadn't been capable
of loyalty. Staring at his daughter, he sees her chest rise and fall
and he is amazed how fiercely loyal she has always been,

despite his inadequacies. Even after the wedding, she had apologized,
not him. And he rebuffed everything, the same way he blocked
her mother. He had compartmentalized all, refusing to see,
as clearly others did, the shell of his life. How under the skin,
he is ugly. And terrified. He is teary again. Her choices
a mystery. Her earnestness. He never knew her, or even her mother.
Take me, he prays. But the words appall him, so made of shadow.

When he sees her he sees her face, her lips, her hands, reminding him how incapable he is. I'm a coward, he thinks, God has never been anything to me, and though for her part she seemingly never doubted now the sums had changed. He knows she wants to die and knows she is more true to her desires than he has ever been to his. True to true desires, she said at one of his firm's corporate functions, and said he was was true too, but only to false desires. Money, cars, women. Even work.

## After the Fallen Angels

All self-consumption. All lies. But so what? You're my father, she said,
I love you. She was drunk. But he'd seen it in her, that love, always.
With her eyes closed she wants to believe him. No ill will, she thinks,
but whenever she goes about town, the whole world seems to watch her
and want to weep, and she feels forced to take from them the invisible
bottles they carry, containers of grief, while she must be silent until she
returns home and lies on her back on the living room floor, the bottles

illumined around her body in the dim light, her own tears like dark rivers
running out from her forever. Weight, a flock of crows clutching
ledges in her room, bed posts, chair backs, black bodies angular
at the foot of the bed, some flapping, some still. People see, but can't
speak, propped up, anesthetized. She'll run. She'll go wherever she
damn well pleases. In the bathroom she lies on the floor. Cold tile. Her
hand reaches, touches the porcelain base of the toilet. Simple. Profound.

Morning again. Tile floor. She sees her father through the doorway.
Again he has sad eyes. His habit of touching two fingers to his temple.
He combs his hands through his hair. He'll be fine, she thinks.
She wonders what will greet her. Nothingness, or tenderness. She isn't
afraid. He won't like another funeral, but she can't worry now. Water
and form, existence. She is formless, she is form without burden, breath,
her bones translucent but dark at the center, like stones under ice.

In seasons of wood or wind, she exists, seamless,
no foresight or alarm, and the cold feeling
that all is arranged to capture and keep her, in wakefulness and sleep,
her thoughts disintegrating and re-collecting.
Alone in her bedroom, she feels no emotion, no anger or even apathy
at him or anyone, no hatred, no sense of panic
or barren expression, no self-annihilation. She stares at the grainy wall,

the surface like landscapes, like mountains and plateaus, steppes,
flatlands, coulees, canyons, flawed as the texture of skin. Love,
she recalls, heals all. She covers her slick face with her hands, covers
her head. She hasn't seen herself for a long time, won't look, would like,
she thinks, never to look again. Late spring, impenetrable fog over
land and sky. A deep quiet below, the river unseen, indifferent bodies
and shiny faces nearby, she knows none of them, this world full of artists.

### After Despair and Courage

This world full of writers, sculptors, painters, poets. The fog
opens and in the haze the river appears far away, broken
into slight white threads that run disjointed to a blue basin where
the water divides again, spilling over rocks and converging finally to one.
She sees trees on the far bank obscured in mist, a stand of cottonwoods,
some aspen. In among the old growth younger trees take form
and as the sun begins to burn they make an image like a silver wing,

or white, or grey. The wing is grey, she decides. Watching her,
he wonders. He takes her hands in his, opens them, touches her fingers.
I'm glad you are here, he says, and she nods and seems to say Yes,
and Thank you, but later he walks the long hall and lifts his head
and sees the open window, a wide and brilliant blue,
and when he pictures her she is fully real
and standing on the sill and when she leans

and walks forward into the air, she kisses the sky.
I am lost, he thinks. Dissolved. Burned. Broken off.
But this time he moves forward and when he climbs
through the window and follows her his dread seeps away.
He reaches her, finds her. Finds himself back where he began.
His daughter, earnestly doing her work beside him.
She lifts her face and looks into his eyes. He finds her beautiful.

# IN THE NEW COUNTRY

Hordes of men struck down, destroyed, sunken form of skin and skeleton, bare cloth matted to torso, bodycage and hipbone, face and neck darkened, bloated to black, rain the endless dream stuck fast in the stone-dead skull and blood a fine sheen over all, arms and legs entwined, a severed hand, eyes dull white opals half-bled from orbital bones, grey earth below and stink in the air and the near cry of predator birds, birds of unbearable hunger, the sodden smell of open wounds, a flock of day raven far above, black, and in the blackness light, black sky with stars and moon like fires defined wholly apart from one another and only darkness in between, mute beacons, and cold. The sun has gone and there is near silence after seven days of fighting, and in the quiet only the caw of birds and the faint word, like a child's, of those whose breath, impatient, labored, severed, stops and takes leave to await them in spirit or etherworld, blood echo on the air, agony awaiting peace on the other side.

# THE GESTURE

*for Jan Palach, son of the Velvet Revolution*

On the surface
he was no exception.

We all cast lots
against the lies of the regime.

Do you agree with the friendly
help of the army?  he asked.

We all answered no
and drew straws

until he nodded,
walked to the public square

and lit the match,
his body

made of
light.

# INVOCATION

### *1*

The truest form
we take is when we are

children. Our bodies swerve
like cliff swallows,

the boy bird with thistle hair
who jumps to touch the sun,

the girl with sound
from her lips like water

from the mountain.
Each of our tears held bright
blue in your hands.

### 2

My wife moves
from the bed

and walks the hall, her hair dark
and light, her body held by her intent.

When she returns she looks wild
as winter, the whole house vivid

in her eyes, and something higher.
Have you ever seen a forest fire

at night,
the world in light so transgressive

the trees breathe
like embers?

*Now*, she whispers,
*They are asleep!*
our three daughters,

and holding my big man's hand she kisses my mouth.
I kissed them too, she says, and I know because I watched

her touch her lips
to the inside of their wrists.

### 3

The height of summer,
her imprint on the rise

of my shoulder sets me on an open plain
with nothing between

us and the end of the world
but grass like tinder, windblown, pale,

and the sun.

*I want to burn*, she says,
and we burn.

# MYSTIC LAKE, THE BEARTOOTH RANGE

This city,
the true city.
The city

of velocity.
The city of want.

The city without nihilism.
This city. The city between

good and evil. City of the
numinous. City of delight.

The real city. This city.
The city of you and I.

The city of nakedness.
The city of dawn.

The city of death.
Yes.

We live in the house
of unspeakable gratitude
in the city of hunger.

# THE FAMILY WHO LIVED
# WITH THEIR FACES TO THE SKY

## *The Big Empty*

Skies run
from a tilted wood porch
all the way
to the horizon
and nothing keeps
back the dawn. Reservation cars, dirty white trucks,
people packed in yellow busses

carting fans to basketball games in midwinter,
sons of trappers
and daughters of sheep shearers,
the blood of a child
in the trunk of an Eldorado,
white crosses in twos or fives
at the bends of this two-lane mountain

are nearly transparent in the backlight.
Everyone here, remains.
People so insignificant they discover God
doesn't owe them anything.
In the deep high country
he is with his father. Grown men now.
And a brother long gone.

Clouds surround the peak up high
to their right, forested at the base,
treeless and rocky at the top
where gold dark eagles fly in dawn's light.

South, the cloudbank thins
and sky reaches
from the ridge

where they stand and look out, down a draw
of scrub pine and mottled veins of sage,
blown timothy grass bent to the ground
and everything converging
along the silver-blue of the big river,
the sweep of the valley,
the four directions, the compass rose,

and far off a land mass: the broad back
of a giant sleeper. The wind comes from the north,
chill and fast from the gap of Canada
down from Glacier over the western mid-Montana plains
to the mountains again, the Beartooths,
the Bridgers, the Spanish Peaks, and blind northeast
behind them the Crazies, cerulean forms

of three plateaus and one high bulk of mountain,
gold mixed among the blue and in the valley shadow
the brown and tan of earth and grasses
bound to riverwater. The land takes them and holds them.
The land delivers them. The only son left alive
contemplates what he sees. You didn't owe us anything, he thinks,
but gave your own beloved.

## The House

He is nine, his brother eleven, summoned
to the relic zone,
their parents' bedroom,
where a mirror plate
trimmed in silver
lies set with their mother's rings
and lead crystal vials of perfume.

The boys sit together
on a blue flowered bedspread
tucked military sharp,
pillows encased and creased
with a hard feminine hand.
The femininity,
the absence of the masculine

surprises and hushes them
because they know the great power
he has over her
and they feel deeply
the façade of this room,
the fear that holds her
here evenings into night

when he mans
the living room and watches TV,
or drives downtown
with alcohol to perform whatever he does
when he's gone, a silence
in the home that is physical.
Her mind is a hot engine

as she lies in the tight curve
of clean sheets and straight coverlet,
her boys breathing, sleeping down the hall.
They've heard her cry so often
they have no words. In that room,
in the afternoon light he is a big man.
Six foot four. Two hundred thirty pounds.

He holds his hands together,
presses his fingers to his forehead. Opens them
again. Bent face and body bent
inward, his shoulders round and chest caved,
his arms surround the cavity
he creates and his hands work the middle
like small animals.

He folds his arms finally,
stands over the boys and says,
Can't seem to make it work.
I'll be going now.
They cry.
He cries.
He leaves.

### The First Definition of Pretty

He comes back
every other Tuesday night,
but ten minutes in she kicks him out,
screams, throws curses
like bombs
as her fists pound dents
in his down green jacket.

She herds him
over the front steps,
down the front walk
to the driveway
as the boys watch
from the window
with their knees on the couch,

their bodies leaned
up the backrest.
Younger brother
touches nose to glass,
sees her face
blown out,
and white teeth shining,

feels
a release of bees
in his stomach
up under the ribcage.
Screen door black and grey,
the words from her mouth ugly,
and older brother

takes him by the hand
and walks him
to the kitchen.
When she returns
she gathers them in her arms,
and sobs. Before now
they had never seen her

hit or cuss. Her husband
never did what she asked
either, but here they
witness him take
every punch like a man
made of glass.
He doesn't look at them

for fear of being
known for what
or who he is, but they watch
and each time they watch they see
him go, and again older brother takes
younger brother's hand and they sit
at the kitchen table and wait.

# The First Definition Of Ugly

Every other Tuesday night. She doesn't attack anymore because he is a teacher and head coach at Plenty Coups, 35 miles south of Billings on the Crow reservation. Be respectable, she tells herself, but out there is where he introduces the boys to his girlfriend. That woman. How young? she asks, and the boys shrug. She looks white but she's mix, they say. She works with him. The games

are at the Shrine Gymnasium, small hot box thick with the smell of people and popcorn and the blond lacquer of hardwood. The players fly—Marty Roundface, Max Spotted Bear, Tim Falls Down and Dana Goes Ahead—and they often win. At home at the oval oak table in the kitchen she sits with her hands folded over like meadow grass.

Is she prettier than me?

The boys race to answer. No, Mom. Never. Not even close.

I don't have to do what you say, the older brother says, and though they'd all thought these words countless times, he was the first to speak them aloud. This, four years after the father returned, left the young woman, remarried their mother. Either sublimation of sexual greed or a kind of family death wish in their father, either his brand of religion or just bad character

made him rigid. She cried in the back of the mobile home, the kind that arrived in two pieces on the flatbeds of 18-wheelers, a step up from the trailer at Bridger and the tiny apartment in Bozeman. The kitchen became the battleground. Younger brother's eighth grade year at St. Labre, school of Northern Cheyenne from Ashland, Lame Deer, and Busby, and Crow bussed in for the week from Lodge Grass

33

and Crow Agency. Late night a black rock, brick-sized, bashed through the window in his parents room. Get down! The father yelled and the boy heard the wheels of a car getting gone, hard floor, open doorway, the father in the shadow of the master bedroom shirtless in tight white underwear as he pointed a rifle out the window. Two months on, no sign of storm. In the house, a more intimate fight. Outside, bunchgrass stood white where the light

waned and far off a wound in the land revealed the rakish tops of cottonwoods in a narrow S naked of leaves above the Powder River, the water muddy brown even in late September. The father never hit the boys but for the familiar swing of the belt. Most often he ruled by volume and the clarity of brutal intention. The night sky nearly violet. The straight edge of the land framing a black void free of stars.

At the center line of the house grey carpet met worn linoleum. Different kitchen, same oak table, same wood chairs, older brother entered the narrow space near the sink and placed his hands on a white Formica counter top graced with gold-yellow grain like small truncated veins. Younger brother left the kitchen, went to the cloth wingback in the living room and curled into the corner of the chair. The door was closed, the windows shut.

## The First Definition of Family

Decrepit house crisp and clean,
the living room pungent with sweat,
younger brother cold watching
older in the fray
as if mauled
or made to fight
for air.
I'm not doing what you say!

Yes, I'm afraid
you will, the father says, eyes rocks
beneath his forehead
as the two approach,
more warships than men,
fists open.
No I won't, older brother says

and puts hands to the father's chest
and shoves him
back. The flush of neck and face.
The image of the father
throwing punches in bars, intoxicated
but intelligent, precise windmills that land
on the skulls of smaller men.

The father lifts the son
from the ground
and slams him
into the nearest oaken midback,
spins the boy to the window and
the purple sky over the cottonwoods splintered
by stars. Shut up, the father yells, and

when he clenches
the boy's white biceps, the boy's eyes go
wet, his face darkens,
his lips tremble.
No! the boy says firmly
but the first slap hits hard
and a white mark blossoms red,

wide, from the center of the cheek
over the cheekbone to the jaw line.
Shut up! the father says again,
I'm telling you.
No.
Skin twitch and body crimp, face swollen,
the son looks neither right nor left,

but stares into his father's eyes
while his mother leans
against the taupe-colored drapes
in the kitchen
and says, Please.
Shut up! the father shouts,
and she moves to the far side of the table

*The People With Their Faces*

and slips
into the living room,
the sheen
of her oldest boy's head,
the rooster flare
of her husband's face,
tears pinching the corners of her eyes
as her hands churn

and her mouth tastes like chalk.
Her husband beats the boy's face
for fifteen minutes straight.
The boy says No
and his father says Shut up
and takes full swings,
open-handed as a flatboard.

He dashes the boy's head
and hair to the side
until the boy,
close-mouthed
with a puffed, blotched face,
sits still
and doesn't cry anymore.

The boy
looks to
his father.
On the command,
Go to your room,
he rises
and walks

past his mother
and younger brother
like something fallen from the sky.
The image
of his shoulders,
the body burned
to white hard bone,

haunts the younger brother
through every wilderness.
The father
follows the boy
from the kitchen
to the end
of the mobile home

and they stay
in the back room.
If the older brother
says a word
the younger hears
nothing. Only wonders
if he is all right,

## To the Sky

wishes for what
isn't there.
There is
no one,
just the island
of a solitary bed,
the grey ceiling, and loneliness.

The father
emerges, goes back
to the kitchen,
makes himself a sandwich
and drinks it down
with a glass
of water.

The older brother remains
face down on the bed,
and the next day
they return to their places:
the father
to his post
as principal,

the two brothers
to school,
their mother
to the linear enclosure
of the mobile home.
In a few short years
the older brother would be gone

into
the maw
of an ancient canyon,
his dark vehicle
burning
in open air
as it leapt the barrier

and fell
far into a valley
black with trees, where
the detonation
boomed and
the forest
bloomed with fire.

And for the rest
of their lives
the older brother spoke
to each one uniquely,
tenderly.
His voice
immutable and holy.

# THREE THINGS GOD DISCERNS

Purity of heart is to will one thing.

—*Søren Kierkegaard*

In the mouths
    of wolves

the tender and
    the dead

find their
    home,

in the wing of an eagle,
    the wind,

on the lips of a lover,
    rough honey.

# A QUIET POEM ABOUT MARITAL SEX

Put your fire to my forest
and pour on oil.

Your gasoline to the struck tip
of the waiting match

and I will stop whatever I'm doing
because in a minute you and I will burn down the world.

Set fire to the pipeline!
See the winter melt in less than sixty seconds,

all the wells of the glittering earth ignite
from underground at once in a thousand sites

and in a thousand cities the beacon fires on the fortified walls
say, We've won!

The gates won't wait for dawn!
They open now!

The tips of your fingers taste like oxygen
and when the torch of my tongue meets you

it's time to drop everything
sit down quietly

and call the handyman
because

we're not worried anymore
about the bills, the yard, the work, the mess—

we're facing what's more pressing . . .
blown the doors off the house.

# THE KITCHEN IN THE AFTERNOON

light sometimes
makes us see each other

as if we were designed
well and with good intention,

my wife and me without
cruelty, the hardwood floor,

the kitchen table, the carpet
in the alcove

next to the oven, the elements,
the S-curves like holy fire

coiled to red
in the easy turn of dusk.

# UP GOING TO THE SUN ROAD, GLACIER NATIONAL PARK, SEPTEMBER, MONTANA, LEAVES LIKE PAPER DOLLS TAPED TO THE FINGERS OF TREES, GOLD-RED, FULL OF LIGHT

### 1

There is nothing to be done
when you've pissed your wife off

and a crazed look comes to her eyes
as she holds a butcher knife

blade up over the onion shoots,
or is there?

### 2

A forty-four year old man approached me.
I was seventeen

and just done eating dinner at his table.
Will you forgive me? he asked.

He said he was wrong to his wife,
and already I had forgotten

his sharp words to her
only ten minutes earlier.

I was on the couch,
eyes glazed with television,

but I looked up, stammered
Yes, you don't have to ask me.

His wife beside him,
his daughter in the distance
the one I would marry.

VI

# EAST OF THE BEAR'S PAW MOUNTAINS,
# NORTH OF MILK RIVER

### *The Hunter's Son*

His father calls him Bull Child,
and bulls he rides, starting at twelve
in the fields of neighboring ranches.
Home, he smells the gun-cleaning, the oil,
the parts in neat rows on the kitchen table made
of rough-hewn wood she drapes in white cloth.
He sees the elongated pipe-cleaner, the blackened rags,

the sheen of rifle barrel,
worn wood of stock, hears
the word Winchester
and how his father speaks it, feels
his father's look downturned,
eyes shadowed, submerged
in the bones.

One-room ranch house. Mother, father, son.
Plankwood floor, eating space,
bed space, cook stove. A small slant-roofed barn stands
east of the house where livestock gather
in the cold. In bed his mother says, Don't make a mess.
The father, meticulous at the table, says, Quiet woman.
Outside, the high plains arc toward Canada.

## Lightning Severs the Arm of the Bear

To the south, wild wind blows
snow to a haze
at the earth's end, and westerly
a rim of sun is red as blood.
She reads aloud by lamplight.
Mind your schooling, she says.
She touches his face.

Her words encompass the world
and he and his father
curl at her feet
on the bed, listening.
Before I formed you in the womb
I knew you, she reads,
and before you were born I set you apart.

Voiceless, they work the land,
the boy in his father's shadow
from the dawn, walking.
The voice of his mother
is what he carries when he goes.
Nineteen, he walks the fence line
in a white out.

Six foot seven, he weighs two hundred fifty pounds.
Along a game trail on the north fence,
two hours from the house
at thirty below zero, he wonders
about his father, gone three days.
His father had come from town, flat look on his face,
sat on the bed and wouldn't eat.

At dark, he'd made a simple pronouncement,
*Getting food*, then gripped the rifle, strode
outside long-legged against the bolt of wind and snow.
Gone, the boy figures and this time the reckoning is true.
Walking, he sees the black barrel of the rifle
angled on the second line of barbed wire,
snow a thin mantle on the barrel's eastward lie.

He sees beneath it the body-shaped mound,
brushes away snow, finds
the frozen head of his father, the open eyes
dull as grey stones.
A small hole under the chin
is burnt around the edges, and at the back
of his father's head, fist-sized, he finds the exit wound.

When the boy pulls the gun from his father's hand
two fingers snap away and land in the snow.
He opens his father's coat, tucks the fingers
in his father's front shirt pocket, shoulders his father,
carries the gun, takes his father home.
Face a tangle of deep-set lines, the boy walks where
the land runs to a sky pale as bone.

*The Hunter*

They place his body
under the kitchen table.
At the grey opening
of dawn
the boy stacks
old tires
out behind the house,

soaks them in gasoline
and lights them,
oily-red pyres
and slanted smoke
columns stark
in the winter quiet.
The ground thaws

as the boy waits.
He spends morning to evening,
using the pick axe,
then the shovel.
Still they bury
the body shallow.
He pushes earth

in over his father,
malformed rock fused
with ice and soil, and when
he's done he pounds the surface
with the flat back of the shovel,
loud bangs blunt and hard
in the cold. The snow

is light now, driven by wind
on a slant from the north.
His mother forms a crude cross
of root wood from the cellar
and the boy manipulates the rock,
positioning the cross
at the head of the grave.

The boy removes
his broken felt cowboy hat,
his gloves. His mother reaches,
holds the boy's hand.
Their faces turn raw in the cold.
Dead now, she says.
Your father saw the world darkly.

And people darker still.
Find the good, boy.
She squeezes the boy's hand,
Dust to dust. May the Good Lord make
the crooked paths straight. May He make
the mountains to be laid low and the valleys
to rise. May he do with the dead as He wills.

*After His Mother Dies*

Alone in the late push
across the borderlands
he rides the Empire Builder
on the Montana Highline.
Rests his hands
on the heel of the shovel,
rests his chin on his hands,

feels the locomotive
spend its light
toward the oncoming darkness,
toward tiny crossings
with unknown names,
towns of eight or ten people.
She has been dead one year now.

He feels the wide wind,
sees the stars
in their opaque immensity.
On the rise toward Glacier,
Wolf Mountain
looms like a bulkhead
in the deep dark.

He hears the long-nosed scream
of the train, bent in the night
and considers
how fully the night
falls, how easily the light
gives way.
He returns to his work

and late he lies himself down
in his sleeping berth
stinking of smoke and oil,
a film of sweat envelops his body
and he falls toward sleep
as one who has come from the earth
and shaped it with his hands,

and here
he hears his mother's voice,
Mind your learning. It is after dinner
when she lays him down,
a child sleeping,
and in the silence
between dark and dawn

she speaks
her elegant words,
presses her cheek
to his, whispers, Awake,
awake, O Zion, clothe yourself in strength.
Put on your garments of splendor.
She smoothes his eyebrow with a forefinger.

## He Wonders at the Light

You can get up now, she says.
She touches his cheek with the back of her hand.
Not yet dawn, he lies on his side.
Sees her ivory hair comb, dull white
on the hard shelf.
Sets the comb in the curve of his hand,
presses the comb to his lips

in the transparent light.
When she died he found a verse
from *Isaiah* in her fingers of bone.
Who has believed our message?
And to whom has the arm of the Lord been revealed?
He breathes,
the memory

of her hand like a circlet over his.
Stares and remembers the smell of her hair.
Moves his index finger along the spine of the comb,
coal and dirt deep set in the whorls.
He draws his finger to his lips.
The sun breaks
the far line of the world.

# ICARUS, USA

There is a highway where dawn is a light on the east Idaho border that illumines Fourth of July and Lookout and carries far, cresting the apex under the blue "Welcome to Montana" sign, riding the downslant to a wilderness more oceanic than earthlike, a manifold vastness of timber, the trees in wide swells that ascend in swaths of shadow and the shadow of shadows until the woodland stops and the vault of sky becomes morning. His older brother alone and in their father's car sped in darkness and blew out the metal guardrail and warped the steel so it reached after the car like a strange hand through which the known world passes, the heavy dark Chevelle like a shot star, headlights that set beams on the night until the chassis turned and the car became an untethered creature that fell and broke itself on the valley floor. Down inside the wreckage, a pale arm from the window. A thin, almost translucent line leading back to what was forsaken. Cold and sudden silence. Then a loud burden from which the night recoiled with fierce incandescent flame.

# SUNFLOWER

## *Little Dry Creek*

When I was a boy my grandma sent me
down to the creek bed for wonders
I'd never find in the city.

Little Dry Creek full of snakes,
Green and yellow striped water-walkers that made
muscular wet coils around my wrist and fingers.

They warmed themselves
and seemed to glow and I felt
the tensile body
we all share
when we are taken under
and when we rise
to find the sun on our skin.

Every Saturday night
my grandmother danced, a whirlwind
on the open plain,
her face in unabated elation
as her laughter harkened
thunderheads and forked lightning.

## She Walks in Darkness

*after Lord Byron*

In the dark before dawn,
when the world waits

and the sky is a burden
in the mountains,

the land, like a hungry animal,
seeks light.

When the day dies
 I want to remember there is nothing

so affirming of my own
death

as the autumn trees
carrying dusk in their arms.

## With My Father

Where the Beartooth Range
navigates southern Montana
we inhabit mountains
and in the predawn black
the darkness stays close,

but when the light begins
lupine and fireweed appear
encased in small intricate robes

of frost and when the sun pierces the sky
and refracts through tiny spheres of water
on each stalk of grass over the high plateau
our feet make a path among stars.

*The Beartooth Highway, Absaroka-Beartooth Wilderness*

Touch my hand
to the hollows and swales,

the rise and fall of your feminine
cathedral made of simple dust.

Touch, so I see
through my unlovely eyes

in the features of your face
I am too often unlovely.

### Van Gogh's Miracle

I want to believe
after death

if we are blessed, I mean
if God chooses,

we will find each other
more lovely than before.

## IN MONTANA

On the river that night
we were in a small boat

open to the stars, no noise
but the big quiet.

This is the gift
God gives, we said,

and did not doubt
how the wilderness

throws its arms on our necks,
our children asleep

in their beds.
Black Mountain on the sky behind you.

Shann Ray has served as a National Endowment for the Arts fellow, a research psychologist for the Centers for Disease Control, a panelist for the National Endowment for the Humanities, Research Division, and a visiting scholar in the Netherlands, the Philippines, Canada, South Africa, and Colombia. His collection of stories, *American Masculine*, named by *Esquire* for their Three Books Every Man Should Read series and selected by *Kirkus Reviews* as a Best Book, won the Bakeless Prize, the High Plains Book Award, and the American Book Award. Sherman Alexie said Ray's work is "tough and beautiful" and Dave Eggers called it "lyrical, prophetic, and brutal, yet ultimately hopeful." Shann's creative nonfiction book of leadership and political theory, *Forgiveness and Power in the Age of Atrocity*, sheds light on the nature of categorical human transgressions and engages the question of ultimate forgiveness in the context of ultimate violence. He is the winner of the *Subterrain* Poetry Prize, the *Crab Creek Review* Fiction Award, the *Poetry Quarterly* Poetry Prize, the *Pacific Northwest Inlander* Short Story Award and the *Ruminate* Short Story Prize. His work has appeared in some of the nation's leading literary venues including *Poetry, McSweeney's, Narrative,* and *Northwest Review.* Shann grew up in Montana and spent part of his childhood on the Northern Cheyenne reservation. He lives with his wife and three daughters, in Spokane, Washington where he teaches leadership and forgiveness studies at Gonzaga University.